本课题受到以下项目资助

◎中国科学院国际合作局项目

“支持 GRC 开放获取行动计划的世界开放获取行动评价与监测平台”（Y140321001）

◎中国科学院科学传播局、发展规划局项目

“中国科学院文献情报和期刊出版领域引进优秀人才计划”择优支持项目（Y14341001）

◎国家自然科学基金委项目

“开放获取重大趋势与科学基金相关政策研究”（ZK16041001）

比菲尔德学术搜索引擎（BASE）简介

Friedrich Summann　主审

顾立平　编

·北京·

图书在版编目（CIP）数据

比菲尔德学术搜索引擎（BASE）简介 / 顾立平编. —北京：科学技术文献出版社，2016. 9（2017. 10 重印）

ISBN 978-7-5189-1881-2

Ⅰ. ①比… Ⅱ. ①顾… Ⅲ. ①学术—搜索引擎—介绍—世界 Ⅳ. ① G254.928

中国版本图书馆 CIP 数据核字（2016）第 215992 号

比菲尔德学术搜索引擎（BASE）简介

策划编辑：崔灵菲　责任编辑：王瑞瑞　责任校对：张吲哚　责任出版：张志平

出 版 者　科学技术文献出版社
地　　址　北京市复兴路15号　邮编 100038
编 务 部　（010）58882938，58882087（传真）
发 行 部　（010）58882868，58882874（传真）
邮 购 部　（010）58882873
官方网址　www.stdp.com.cn
发 行 者　科学技术文献出版社发行　全国各地新华书店经销
印 刷 者　虎彩印艺股份有限公司
版　　次　2016 年 9 月第 1 版　2017 年 10 月第 3 次印刷
开　　本　850 × 1168　1/32
字　　数　51千
印　　张　3.125
书　　号　ISBN 978-7-5189-1881-2
定　　价　38.00元

前 言

比菲尔德学术搜索引擎（Bielefeld Academic Search Engine，BASE）是世界级海量内容的搜索引擎之一，专注于学术信息开放获取的网络资源，对所有用户免费开放。它具有如下特点：①智能化资源选择；②只收录符合学术质量的文件；③提供用户搜索的透明性；④深入“底层网页”资源；⑤搜索结果会显示之前的文献数据；⑥具有多个选项来排序搜索结果；⑦具有“分层分页”的搜索选项；⑧能够以DDC（杜威十进分类法）和文件类型进行浏览。本书介绍如何使用、如何加入资源，以及 BASE 的基本原理。

本书简要介绍 BASE 的发展与成就，分析了其相对商业搜索引擎所独有的特点。关于其使用，简要介绍用户的基本使用方式，包括浏览、同义词 / 翻译语、博客 / 推客、移动通信设备的网页、搜索插件等；介绍 BASE 为数据库和知识库管理者服务的具体步骤，包括整合 BASE 到本地基础设施，注册 IP 位置、测试和使用界面等；结合具体实际解答了关于 BASE 的各种问题，如针对 BASE 概述、索引 / 内容来源、搜索 / 命中列表、BASE 网站等方面的问题。本书最后给出对 BASE 各种操作的中文版界面截图，并介绍了 BASE HTTP 接口，详细介绍了所支持的 3 种方法的语法和案例，方便读者理解。全书中英德 3 种文字结合，帮助全面认识 BASE 的组织、功能、已有成果、发展方向等。

本书知识内容的贡献者是 Friedrich Summann 先生。顾立平负责 BASE 中文版界面的编译、本书内容编译，以及本书编纂；最终稿件由 Friedrich Summann 主审。协助本书内容完成的人员还有：吴蓉测试 BASE 中文官网、杨良斌通读本书全文、史盈盈和丁利芳参与编辑等。

Inhalt

Content

目　录

1 Über BASE

>>>>>>>>>>>>>>>>>>>>>>>>>>>>

1.1 Einleitung

BASE (Bielefeld Academic Search Engine) ist eine der weltweit größten Suchmaschinen für wissenschaftliche Web-Dokumente. Betreiber der Suchmaschine BASE ist die Universitätsbibliothek Bielefeld.

BASE sammelt die Metadaten wissenschaftlicher Dokumente, die über das OAI-PMH-Protokoll bereitgestellt werden. Der Index umfasst über 90 Millionen Dokumente aus über 4.000 Quellen.

Bei etwa 60% der in BASE indexierten Dokumente sind die Volltexte frei zugänglich (Open Access).

Der Index wird durch Aufnahme weiterer Quellen kontinuierlich ausgebaut. Daneben arbeiten wir an verschiedenen Weiterentwicklungen, z.B. dem Aufbau eines Claiming-Dienstes für Autoren (Projekt ORCID DE).

BASE ist registrierter OAI-Service-Provider. Datenbankbetreiber können den BASE-Index über Schnittstellen in eigene Anwendungen

(Metasuchmaschinen, Bibliothekskataloge) integrieren. Darüber hinaus bieten wir viele weitere Tools und Services für Anwender, Datenbank- und Repository-Betreiber an.

1.2 Merkmale der

Im Vergleich zu kommerziellen Suchmaschinen zeichnen BASE folgende Merkmale aus:

① Intellektuelle Auswahl der indexierten Quellen.

② Exklusive Berücksichtigung fachlicher qualifizierter Dokumentenserver.

③ Transparenz der durchsuchten Datenquellen über ein entsprechendes Quellenverzeichnis.

④ Erschließung von Internetquellen des "Unsichtbaren Web", die in kommerziellen Suchmaschinen nicht indexiert werden oder in deren großen Treffermengen untergehen.

⑤ Korrektur, Normalisierung und Anreicherung von Metadaten mit Hilfe automatisierter Verfahren.

⑥ Präsentation der Suchergebnisse mit differenzierter Anzeige von bibliographischen Daten.

⑦ Anzeige von Zugangs- und Nachnutzungsmöglichkeiten zu einem Dokument.

⑧ Unterschiedliche Optionen zur Sortierung der Trefferliste.

⑨ Suchverfeinerung nach Autoren, Schlagwörtern, DDC-Klassifikation, Erscheinungsjahren, Quellen, Sprachen, Dokumentart, Zugang und Nachnutzung.

⑩ Browsing nach DDC-Klassifikation und Dokumentart.

2 Für Anwender

2.1 Browsing

0 Informatik, Informationswissenschaft,
1 Philosophie und Psychologie (561597)
2 Religion (184167)
3 Sozialwissenschaften (2767784)

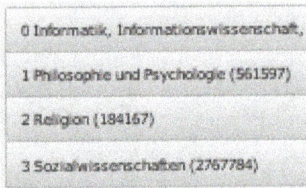

Über das Browsing finden Sie Dokumente ganz ohne Suchmaske. Die Dokumente sind nach Dewey-Dezimal-Klassifikation (DDC), Dokumentart, Lizenz oder Zugangsart geordnet.

BASE-Browsing starten.

2.2 Synonyme / Übersetzungen

klimatologie
Exakte Suche
Zusätzliche Wortformen
Synonyme (Eurovoc The

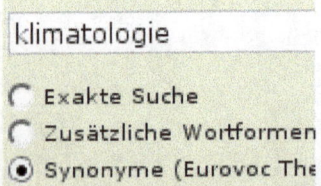

Multilinguale Suche mit dem Eurovoc Thesaurus: Über den

Punkt "Synonyme" können Sie gleichzeitig nach Synonymen und Übersetzungen suchen. Eurovoc umfasst 239.000 Einträge in 21 Sprachen.

Beispielsuche mit Thesaurus.

2.3 Blog / Twitter

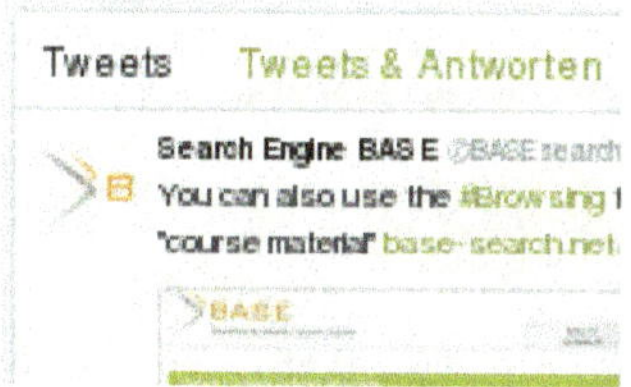

Unser BASE Weblog informiert über Neuerungen in BASE. Folgen Sie uns auf unserem Twitter-Kanal@BASEsearch. Wenn Sie selbst über BASE twittern möchten verwenden Sie am besten das Hashtag #basesearch.

2.4 Mobile Website

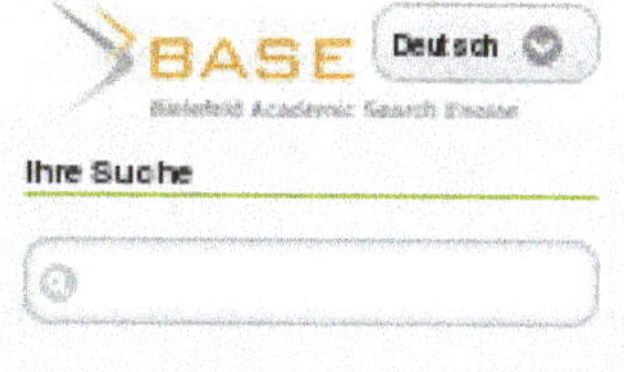

Smartphone-Clients werden automatisch auf die BASE-Mobil-

Seiten umgeleitet. BASE unterstützt alle gängigen Plattformen (Android, IOS, Windows Phone, u.a.).

Zur mobilen Website.

2.5 Search Plugin

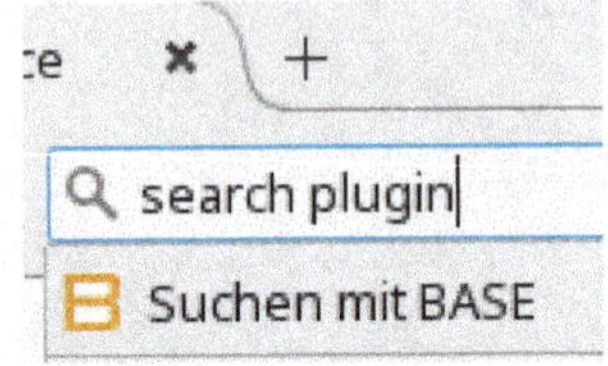

Schneller suchen mit dem BASE Search Plugin (fürChrome, Firefox und Internet Explorer). Durchsuchen Sie das wissenschaftliche Internet mit BASE direkt über die Suchmaschinen-Toolbar in Ihrem Browser.

Search Plugin für BASE installieren.

2.6 Suchbox

Fügen Sie folgenden Quelltext in Ihre eigene Webseite ein, um eine Suchmaske für die Suche in BASE zu erstellen:

<form action="https://www.base-search.net/Search/Results" method="get" accept-charset="UTF-8">

```
<input type="text" name="lookfor" style="width:200px;" maxlength="1024" />
<input type="submit" value="Suche in BASE"/>
<input type="hidden" name="l" value="de"/>
<input type="hidden" name="refid" value="dcexternde" />
</form>
```

Per CSS können Sie das Aussehen der Suchmaske natürlich ändern und ggf. an Ihr Design anpassen (verändern Sie nicht den Quelltext, da dies die Funktionalität beeinträchtigen kann).

2.7 Zotero-Schnittstelle

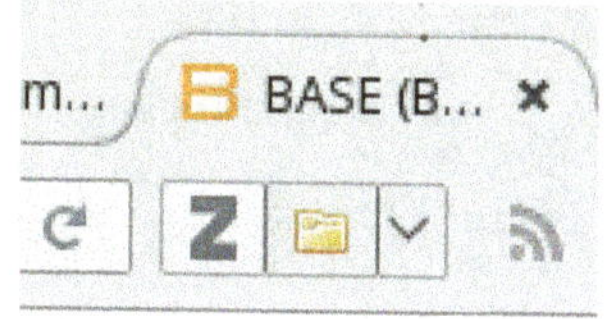

Zotero ist ein plattformunabhängiges Open-Source-Programm zum Sammeln, Verwalten und Zitieren unterschiedlicher Online- und Offline-Quellen, das direkt als Erweiterung ("Add-on") im Firefox-Browser genutzt wird. Die Funktionen einer "klassischen" Literaturverwaltung werden weitgehend unterstützt. Nach Installation des Add-Ons können Sie Titel ausBASE in Zotero übernehmen.

Zotero herunterladen.

3 Für Datenbank- und Repository-Betreiber

3.1 Integration von BASE in eigene Anwendungen

```
<response>
 -<lst name="responseH
    <int name="status">
    <int name="QTime">
   -<lst name="params"
     -<str name="fl">
        dccollection,dccont
```

Sie können den BASE-Index in eigene Anwendungen (z.B. Metasuchmaschinen, Bibliothekskataloge) über eine HTTP-Schnittstelle integrieren:Anleitung zur Verwendung der BASE-Schnittstelle (Version 1.9, Juni 2016).

Bevor Sie die Schnittstelle testen und verwenden können, muss Ihre IP-Adresse freigeschaltet werden. Schreiben Sie uns dazu bitte eine kurzeNachricht.

3.2 BASE OAI-Schnittstelle


```
<OAI-PMH xsi:schemaLoca
  <responseDate>2014-09-
  <request verb="ListRecor
- <ListRecords>
  - <record>
    - <header>
        <identifier>ftciteseer
```


Projektpartner können den BASE-Index auch über eine OAI-PMH-Schnittstelle abrufen:

BASE OAI Interface.

Bevor Sie die Schnittstelle testen und verwenden können, muss Ihre IP-Adresse freigeschaltet werden. Schreiben Sie uns dazu bitte eine kurzeNachricht.

3.3 OAI-Schnittstelle validieren

OVAL, der BASE OAI-PMH Validity Checker testet schnell und einfach OAI-Schnittstellen auf ihre Kompatibilität zu BASE.

3.4 OAI-PMH-Weblog

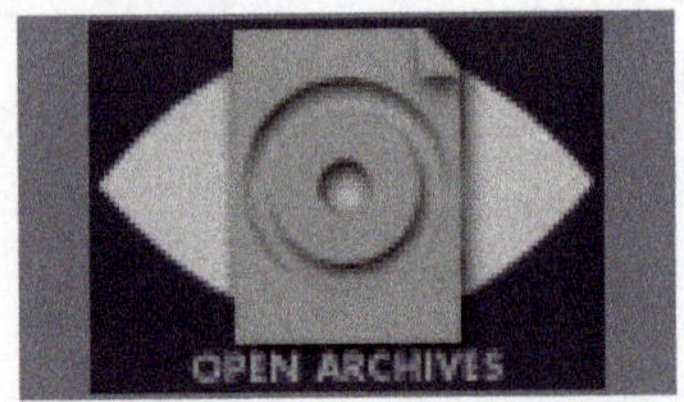

Unser OAI-PHM-Blog informiert über unsere Aktivitäten in Bezug auf Harvesting und Aggegration von Metadaten.

4 FAQ

4.1 Allgemeine Fragen zu BASE

(1) Was ist BASE?

BASE (Bielefeld Academic Search Engine) ist eine der weltweit größten Suchmaschinen für wissenschaftliche Open-Access-Dokumente, z.B. Zeitschriftenartikel, Preprints oder Dissertationen. Probieren Sie BASE direkt aus: Suche mit BASE starten.

(2) Was ist BASE Lab?

Neue Suchmöglichkeiten, Tools und Tests werden regelmäßig im BASE Lab vorgestellt, auf die wir in unserem Weblog und Twitter-Kanal hinweisen: Ins BASE Labgehen.

(3) Was unterscheidet BASE von allgemeinen Internetsuchmaschinen?

Mit BASE finden Sie viele wissenschaftliche Internetquellen, die in Suchmaschinen wie Google oder Bing nicht zu finden sind oder in deren riesigen Treffermengen untergehen. Die durchsuchten Quellen werden intellektuell ausgewählt und geprüft. Datenmüll und

Suchmaschinen-Spam gibt es in BASE nicht. Lesen Sie die weiteren Informationen zum Projekt.

（4） Wer steckt hinter BASE?

BASE ist ein Projekt der Universitätsbibliothek Bielefeld: Das BASE-Team stellt sich vor.

（5） Wie sieht die Zukunft von BASE aus?

BASE wird als strategisches Projekt der Universitätsbibliothek Bielefeld fortlaufend weiterentwickelt.

（6） Wo kann ich Lob, Kritik und Anregungen loswerden?

Schreiben Sie uns, was Sie von BASE halten über unser Kontaktformular, schreiben Sie einen Kommentar in unserem Blog oder twittern Sie mit dem Hashtag#basesearch.

4.2 Fragen zur Indexierung und zur Aufnahme neuer Quellen

（1） Welche Indexierungssoftware wird für BASE verwendet?

Im BASE-System wird seit Mai 2011 die Open-Source-Technologie von Solr/Lucene verwendet. Bis Mai 2011 wurde die Suchmaschinentechnolgie von Microsoft FAST (Fast Search And Transfer) verwendet.

（2） Nach welchen Kriterien werden neue Quellen für BASE

ausgewählt?

Wir indexieren grundsätzlich die Inhalte wissenschaftlicher Quellen, die Ihre Metadaten über OAI-PMH bereitstellen (Repositorien / OAI-Server). Wir untersuchen regelmäßig Repository-Verzeichnisse wie zum Beispiel OpenArchives, ROAR und OpenDOAR oder die Listen entsprechender Software-Installationen wie z.B. DSpaceoder OJS auf neue Quellen und harvesten (einsammeln) die Inhalte geeigneter Quellen. Anschließend werden die Quellen indexiert.

(3) Wie kann ich eine neue Quelle vorschlagen?

Wenn Sie Betreiber eines Repositories/E-Journals mit wissenschaftlichen Inhalten sind und Ihre Quelle weder in unserer Quellenliste noch über die Suche gefunden haben, benutzen Sie unser Kontaktformular und teilen Sie uns den Namen des Repositories, die URL der Startseite (Weboberfläche) und die Basis-URL der OAI-Schnittstelle mit. Wir werden die Daten umgehend prüfen und Ihnen Rückmeldung geben, ob eine Indexierung möglich ist.

Auch wenn Sie nicht selbst Betreiber eines Dokumentenservers sind, können Sie uns jederzeit eine neue Quelle vorschlagen. Die Quelle muss wissenschaftliche Dokumente enthalten und sollte diese möglichst frei im Volltext anbieten. Senden Sie uns über das

Kontaktformular den Namen und die URL der Quelle und - falls bekannt - die Adresse der OAI-Schnittstelle. Wir werden die Quelle prüfen, ob sie unseren technischen und qualitativen Vorgaben entspricht und Ihnen so schnell wie möglich Rückmeldung geben.

(4) Wie richtige ich eine OAI-Schnittstelle ein, damit mein Repository/E-Journal von BASE indexiert werden kann?

Auf der Website der Open Archives Initiative finden Sie eine Anleitung zum Aufsetzen einer OAI-Schnittstelle. Allgemeine Informationen zu OAI finden Sie bei openarchives.org und in der Wikipedia. Mit unserem OAI-Validator OVAL können Sie Ihre OAI-Schnittstelle auf Kompatiblität zu BASE prüfen und feststellen ob es noch Probleme gibt.

Handelt es sich bei Ihrer Quelle um eine Open-Access-Zeitschrift, genügt es auch, wenn Sie Ihre Zeitschrift im "Directory of Open Access Journals" eintragen. Da wir die Inhalte des DOAJ indexieren und regelmäßig aktualisieren, wird somit auch Ihre Zeitschrift automatisch nach einiger Zeit von uns indexiert und ist in BASE zu finden. Informationen zur Aufnahme einer Zeitschrift ins DOAJ finden Sie in der DOAJ-FAQ.

Eine weitere Möglichkeit ist die Verwendung des Open Journal Systems (OJS), mit dem sich Online-Zeitschriften (auch solche, die nicht Open-Access sind) recht einfach verwalten lassen. Das

System ist Open Source und kostenlos und verfügt auch über eine eingebaute OAI-Schnittstelle. E-Journals, die über OJS angeboten werden, werden von uns bevorzugt indexiert. Weitere Informationen zu OJS.

(5) Wie oft werden die Inhalte indexierter Quellen im BASE-Index aktualisiert?

Die Inhalte bereits indexierter Dokumentenserver werden in aller Regel jedes Wochenende aktualisiert und ergänzt. In größen Abständen werden die Inhalte vollständig neu geholt ("reharvested").

(6) Warum sind manche Quelle unvollständig oder einzelne Dokumente offenbar fehlerhaft indexiert?

Zu unvollständig indexierten Quellen oder fehlerhaft indexierten Dokumente kommt es in aller Regel, wenn es Probleme mit der OAI-Schnittstelle der Quelle gibt. In der Weboberfläche einer Quelle kann dabei durchaus alles korrekt sein, da wir aber nur die OAI-Metadaten indexieren ist die Anzeige der Weboberfläche für die Indexierung in BASE nicht relevant. Fehler können Sie uns jederzeit über das Kontaktformular mitteilen. Wenn Sie der Betreiber der Quelle sind überprüfen Sie bitte auch Ihre OAI-Schnittstelle mit unserem OAI-Validator OVAL.

(7) Werden Quellen auch aus dem BASE-Index wieder

entfernt?

Wir überprüfen alle indexierten Quellen regelmäßig. Quellen, deren Server oder OAI-Schnittstellen über einen längeren Zeitraum gar nicht oder nur sehr unzuverlässig arbeiten oder die keine Open-Access-Inhalte mehr anbieten, werden aus dem Index temporär oder dauerhaft entfernt.

4.3 Fragen zur Suche und zur Trefferliste

（1）Wie suche ich in BASE?

Eine Anleitung zur Recherche und zur Trefferliste finden Sie in unserer Hilfe.

（2）Ist eine Suche im gesamten Text der indexierten Dokumente möglich?

BASE indexiert aus Zeit- und Kapatizitätsgründen nur die Metadaten (Titel, Abstract...) von Dokumenten, aber nicht den gesamten Volltext. Daher ist eine Suche im gesamten Text der indexierten Dokumente nicht möglich.

（3）Kann ich meine Suche auf Open-Access-Dokumente einschränken?

Sie können in der erweiterten Suche unter “Zugang” die Suche auf Open-Access-Dokumente einschränken bzw. Dokumente, die nicht frei zugänglich sind, ausschließen. Außerdem können Sie hier auch direkt auf CC-Lizenzen (Creative Commons) einschränken. CC-Lizenzen ermöglichen, die Weiterverbreitung der Inhalte - dabei gibt es verschiedene Unter-Lizenzen, je nachdem, ob z.B. eine kommerzielle Weiterverbreitung erlaubt ist oder ob die Weiterverbreitung ebenfalls unter einer CC-Lizenz erfolgen muss. Näheres erfahren Sie z.B. in der Wikipedia.

Sie können auch nach einer Recherche in der Trefferliste das Suchergebnis auf Open-Access-Dokumente eingrenzen. Klicken Sie dazu im Bereich "Suchergebnis eingrenzen" auf "Zugang" und dann auf "Freier Zugang (Open Access)". Das Suchergebnis wird dann auf Dokumente eingegrenzt, die von den Datenlieferanten eindeutig als Open Access gekennzeichnet wurden. Einige Datenlieferanten liefern keine oder unzureichende Informationen über den Zugang, daher konnten wir bisher nur etwa 30% der Dokumente als eindeutig Open Access kennzeichnen (insgesamt sind etwa 60% der indexierten Dokumente frei zugänglich).

(4) Warum erhalte ich keinen Zugriff auf den Volltext eines Dokuments?

Die Metadaten aller indexierten Dokumente können über BASE durchsucht werden. Bei etwa 60% der in BASE indexierten Dokumente sind die Volltexte frei zugänglich (Open Access), die restlichen 30% sind Dokumente ohne Volltext oder Dokumente, bei denen der Volltext nicht frei zugänglich ist. Ist der Volltext nicht frei zugänglich, können Sie auf den Inhalt, also zum Beispiel auf den Volltext eines Aufsatzes, nur zugreifen, wenn Sie für den Zugriff autorisiert sind. Dies ist zum Beispiel der Fall, wenn Ihre Institution (Universität, Firma...) eine Lizenz für den Zugriff besitzt und Ihr PC für den Zugriff freigeschaltet wurde. Die Lizenzkontrolle wird ausschließlich vom Datenlieferanten vorgenommen. Falls Sie keinen Zugriff auf einen Volltext erhalten sollten, obwohl Ihre Institution eine Lizenz besitzt, wenden Sie sich daher bitte direkt an Ihre EDV-Abteilung oder an den Datenlieferanten.

(5) Warum kann ich auf ein Dokument, dass als “Open Access” gekennzeichnet, nicht zugreifen?

Sollte ein Dokument als “Open Access” gekennzeichnet sein, das Dokument aber dennoch nicht zugänglich sein, liegt in der Regel ein Fehler beim Betreiber vor. Wir kennzeichnen Dokumente als “Open Access” gemäß der Angaben, die wir vom Betreiber erhalten (z.B. entsprechende Angabe in den Rechteinformationen oder vorliegen einer sogenannten CC-Lizenz). Wir können nicht individuell inhaltlich prüfen, ob diese Angaben korrekt sind. Sollten Sie auf ein Dokument stoßen, dass nicht korrekt als “Open Access” gekennzeichnet ist, wenden Sie sich am besten direkt an den

Datenlieferanten und weisen ihn auf das Problem hin.

(6) Waum erhalte ich beim Zugriff auf ein Dokument eine Fehlermeldung?

Erhalten Sie eine 404-Fehlermeldung ("Seite nicht gefunden") kann es sein, dass sich die Internetadresse des Dokuments seit der letzten Indexierung verändert hat oder dass das Dokument aus dem Repository gelöscht wurde. Zwar sollen Inhalte aus wissenschaftlichen Repositorien mit nicht-veränderlichen Adressen ausgestattet sein und Änderungen und Löschungen über die OAI-Schnittstelle des Datenlieferanten mitgeteilt werden, in der Praxis ist dies jedoch nicht immer der Fall. Daher kommt es auch immer wieder vor, dass Links auf Dokumente aus unserer Trefferliste heraus nicht mehr funktionieren. Ein weiterer Grund für eine Fehlermeldung kann sein, dass der Server des Repositories temporär oder dauerhaft nicht erreichbar ist. Sollte Ihnen ein Fehler auffallen, teilen Sie uns dies einfach über unser Kontaktformular mit. Wir werden dann den Betreiber über den Fehler informieren oder die Quelle aus dem Index entfernen, wenn es sich um ein dauerhaftes Problem handelt.

(7) Was sind Metadaten?

Insbesondere im wissenschaftlichen Bereich verfügen Dokumente oft über so genannte Metadaten. Dies sind Angaben die das Dokument formal und/oder inhaltlich beschreiben. Zu den Metadaten gehören, neben dem Titel, z.B. Autorennamen, Erscheinungsdatum, Inhaltsbeschreibung, Sprache oder bei Zeitschriftenaufsätzen Informationen zum Titel und zur Ausgabe der Zeitschrift. Die von uns indexierten Quellen verfügen über solche Metadaten, daher können Sie in der erweiterten Suche gezielt nach Autoren oder Erscheinungsjahren suchen oder in der Trefferliste Ihr Suchergebnis gezielt darauf einschränken. “Normale” Internetseiten verfügen dagegen in aller Regel nicht über diese Metadaten, daher ist auch eine gezielte Suche nach Autoren oder Erscheinungsjahren in Internetsuchmaschinen wie Google oder Bing nicht oder nur fehlerhaft möglich.

(8) Die Metadaten sind fehlerhaft. Kann man das korrigieren?

Wenn Sie Fehler in den Metadaten in einem Treffer entdecken, z.B. falsche oder fehlende Autorennamen, Titel, Jahreszahlen oder Fehler im Zeichensatz (z.B. ? statt eines Buchstabens), sind hierfür die Betreiber verantwortlich. Wir korrigieren bereits bei der Indexierung offensichtliche Fehler in den Metadaten mit automatisierten Verfahren, jedoch ist eine inhaltliche Prüfung unmöglich. Wenden Sie sich am besten direkt an den Datenlieferanten, wenn Sie in einem Datensatz fehler entdecken.

Sollte der Datensatz beim Datenlieferanten korrekt erscheinen, kann es sein, dass die Daten fehlerhaft über die OAI-Schnittstelle ausgeliefert werden, welche wir für die Indexierung der Daten verwenden. Es kann auch sein, dass der Datensatz vom Betreiber kürzlich korrigiert wurde. In diesem Fall werden die Daten auch in der BASE-Trefferliste bei der nächsten Indexierung (i.d.R. innerhalb von 1-2 Wochen) korrigiert.

4.4 Fragen zu den BASE-Webseiten

(1) Wieso erscheinen die BASE-Webseiten bei mir standardmäßig nicht in deutsch?

Die Seiten (Suchmasken, Infoseiten) werden Ihnen in der Sprache angezeigt, die in Ihrem Browser voreingestellt ist. Diese Voreinstellungen können Sie im Browser ändern. Stellen Sie dort "Deutsch" als bevorzugte Sprache ein. Die BASE-Seiten werden ab sofort standardmäßig in deutsch angezeigt. Natürlich können Sie auch über die Auswahlbox rechts oben auf jeder Seite die Sprache wechseln.

(2) Gibt es eine Druckversion Ihrer Seiten?

Die BASE-Webseiten sind so gestaltet, dass Sie beim Ausdruck automatisch eine für den Ausdruck optimierte Fassung erhalten.

(3) Gibt es eine Version für mobile Endgeräte (Smartphones etc.)?

Ja. Wenn Sie mit einem mobilen Endgerät auf BASE zugreifen, werden Sie automatisch zur mobilen Version umgeleitet. Die mobile Version können Sie auch unter m.base-search.net aufrufen.

(4) Muss Javascript, Java oder ähnliches in meinem Browser aktiviert sein?

Nein. Auf den BASE-Webseiten wird zwar an einigen Stellen Javascript verwendet, die Seiten sind aber so gestaltet, dass alle Funktionen auch ohne Javascript genutzt werden können.

(5) Erfüllen die BASE-Seiten Webstandards?

Ja. Die BASE-Webseiten sind grundsätzlich so gestaltet, dass sie mit allen Browsern und allen Betriebssystemen ohne Einschränkungen genutzt werden können. Die Seiten sind gemäß Webstandards (XHTML, CSS) erstellt. Ältere Browser (zum Beispiel Netscape 4), die aktuelle Webstandards nicht beherrschen, erhalten eine Textfassung ohne besonderes Layout.

Großer Wert wurde darauf gelegt, dass die Anforderungen für barrierefreie Webseiten nach der BITV (Barrierefreie Informationstechnik-Verordnung) möglichst vollständig erfüllt werden.

(6) Warum sind einige Wörter unterstrichelt dargestellt?

Akronyme und Abkürzungen wie zum Beispiel das Wort

BASE werden bei ihrem ersten Auftreten im Text einer Seite mit einer Erläuterung versehen. Diese wird angezeigt, wenn Sie den Mauszeiger über das Wort platzieren. Damit Sie erkennen können, wo das Wort erstmals erläutert wird, ist das Wort an dieser Stelle unterstrichelt dargestellt.

1 About BASE

1.1 Brief Introduction

BASE is one of the world's most voluminous search engines especially for academic web resources. BASE is operated by Bielefeld University Library.

BASE collects and indexes the metadata of web documents, provided via the OAI-PMH protocol. BASE provides more than 90 million documents from more than 4,000 sources.

You can access the full texts of about 60% of the indexed documents for free (Open Access).

The index is continuously enhanced by integrating further sources. We are working on several new features like a claiming service for authors (ORCID DE project).

BASE is a registered OAI service provider. Database managers can integrate the BASE index into their local infrastructure (e.g. meta search engines, library catalogues). Further on there are several tools and services for users, database and repository managers.

1.2 Features

In comparison to commercial search engines, BASE is characterised by the following features:

① Intellectually selected resources.

② Only document servers that comply with the specific requirements of academic quality and relevance are included.

③ A data resources inventory provides transparency in the searches.

④Discloses web resources of the "Deep Web", which are ignored by commercial search engines or get lost in the vast quantity of hits.

⑤ Correction, normalization and enrichment of metadata by means of automated methods.

⑥ The display of search results includes precise bibliographic data.

⑦ Display of access and terms of re-use for a document.

⑧ Several options for sorting the result list.

⑨ "Refine your search result" options (by author, subject, DDC, year of publication, content provider, language, document type, access and terms of re-use).

⑩ Browsing by DDC (Dewey Decimal Classification), document type, access and terms of re-use / licence.

2 Services for Users

2.1 Browsing

0 Computer science, information &
1 Philosophy & psychology (56159
2 Religion (184167)
3 Social sciences (2767784)

Find documents without typing search terms. You can choose from two kinds of browsing, by Dewey Decimal Classification (DDC) and by document type.

Start browsing BASE.

2.2 Synonyms / Translations

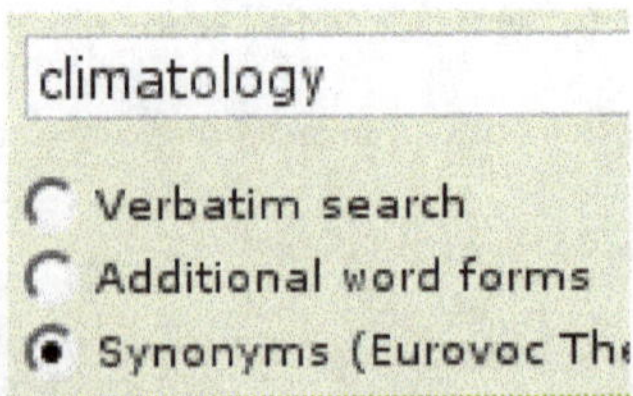

Multi-lingual search with Eurovoc thesaurus: By choosing

"Multilingual Synonyms" you can search for synonyms and translations. All in all 239,000 terms from 21 languages are included in Eurovoc.

Search with Eurovoc.

2.3 Blog / Twitter

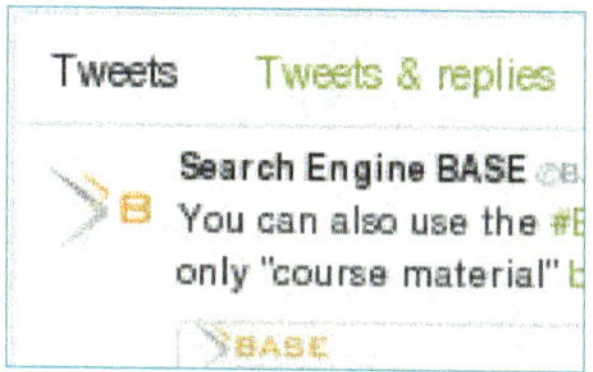

Follow us on our twitter channel@BASEsearch. If you like to twitter about BASE you can use the hashtag#basesearch. On our Weblog you can get general news about BASE (in German only).

2.4 Website for Mobile Devices

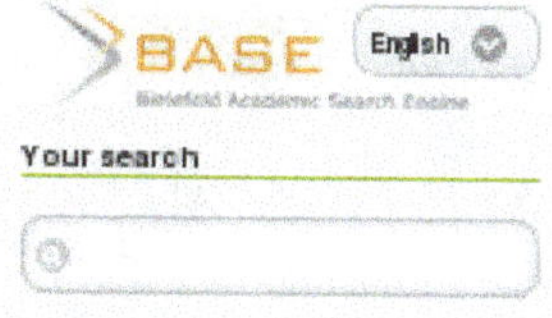

Smartphone clients will be automatically redirected to our

mobile website. BASE supports all modern platforms like Android, IOS, Windows Phone.

Access mobile website.

2.5 Search Plugin

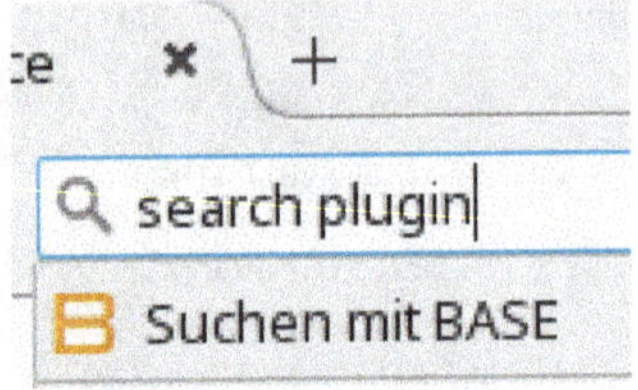

Search faster with the BASE search plugin (for Firefox 2 and higher and IE7 and higher). You can search the academic web with BASE directly through the search toolbar of your browser.

Install BASE search plugin.

2.6 Search Box

If you want to provide a search field for BASE searches on your website, simply add the following piece of source code to your home page:

<form action="http://www.base-search.net/Search/Results" method="get" accept-charset="UTF-8">

```
<input type="text" name="lookfor" style="width:200px;" maxlength="1024" />
<input type="submit" value="Search BASE" />
<input type="hidden" name="l" value="en" />
<input type="hidden" name="refid" value="dcexternen" />
</form>
```

By using CSS you can customize the design of the search box, so that it fits your web site well. Be careful not to modify the code, it may affect the functionality.

2.7 Interface for Zotero

Zotero is the name of a platform independent open source software for collecting, managing and citing various kinds of online and offline resources. It is available and useable as an add-on for the Firefox browser. To a large extent, the assumed functions of a classic reference management system are supported. After having installed the add-on you can transfer results from BASE to Zotero.

Download Zotero.

3 For Database and Repository Manager

3.1 Integration of BASE into Local Infrastructures


```
<response>
–<lst name="responseH
   <int name="status">
   <int name="QTime">
  –<lst name="params"
    –<str name="fl">
       dccollection,dccont
```


You can integrate the BASE index into your own local infrastructure (e.g. meta search engines, library catalogues). For the realisation we provide a HTTP interface. A manual is available for download: Download BASE Interface Guide (Version 1.9, June 2016).

Before you can start testing and using the interface, your IP address needs to be registered first. Please send us a short message.

3.2 BASE OAI Interface


```
<OAI-PMH xsi:schemaLoca
  <responseDate>2014-09-
  <request verb="ListRecor
–<ListRecords>
  –<record>
    –<header>
       <identifier>ftciteseei
```

Project partners can retrieve the OAI metadata collected and normalized by BASE via an OAI-OMH interface:

BASE OAI interface.

Before you can start testing and using the interface, your IP address needs to be registered first. Please send us a short message.

3.3 Validate OAI Interface

A service for repository managers: OVAL, the BASE OAI-PMH Validity Checker easily verifies if the OAI-interface is compliant with the BASE requirements.

3.4 OAI-PMH Blog

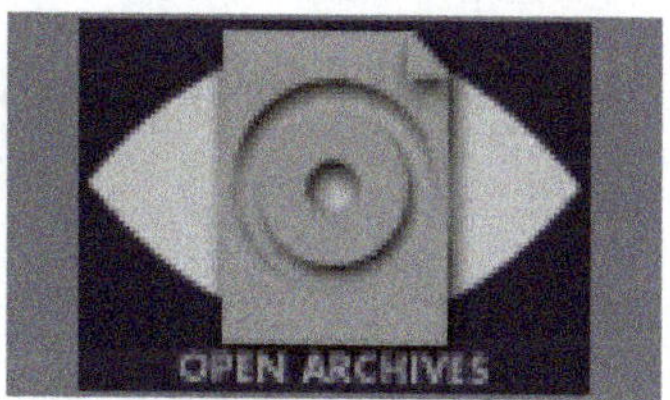

Our OAI-PHM Blog communicates information related to harvesting and aggregating activities performed for BASE.

4 FAQ

4.1 BASE in General

(1) What is BASE?

BASE is one of the world's most voluminous search engines especially for academic open access web resources. BASE is operated by Bielefeld University Library. Try searching with BASE right now!

(2) What is BASE Lab?

New features and tools will be presented in the BASE Lab first. Check our Blog or Twitter channel to stay up to date.

(3) What is Different about BASE?

BASE facilitates effective and targeted searches and retrieves high quality, academically relevant results. Other than search engines like Google or Bing BASE searches the deep web as well. The sources which are included in BASE are intellectually selected and reviewed. That's why data garbage and spam do not occur. Read more details about the project.

(4) The People Behind BASE

BASE represents a project of Bielefeld University: The BASE Team.

(5) BASE Future Developments

The strategic project BASE is in a state of constant development.

(6) Get in Touch With Us!

We highly appreciate your comments and feedback. Leave us a message, write a comment in our blog or twitter using the hash tag #basesearch.

4.2 Indexing / Content Sources

(1) Which indexing software is used for BASE?

Since May 2011 we are using the open source search technology of Solr/Lucene. Until May 2011 the search engine technology of Microsoft FAST (Fast Search And Transfer) was used.

(2) Which criteria do new sources have to meet to be added to the BASE index?

We are indexing all kinds of academically relevant material from content sources which use the "Open Archives Initiative Protocol for Metadata Harvesting" (OAI-PMH) for providing their metadata. We observe several repository directories like OpenArchives, ROAR and OpenDOAR or repository software directories like DSpace or OJS regularly and harvest and index the content of sources.

(3) How can I recommend a new content source?

If you are a repository manager or an editor of an academic e-journal and you couldn't find your content source neither in our list of content sources nor via a search in our index, let us know the name of your repository, the URL of the repository's home page and the basic URL of the OAI interface via our contact form. We will check the data immediately and give you feedback, if it's possible to index your content source.

Even if you are not a repository manager you may suggest new content sources anytime. The source has to contain academic documents and should offer full texts for free (open access). Send us the name and the URL and - if possible - the basic URL of the OAI interface via our contact form. We will check if the content source fits our scope and give you feedback.

(4) How do I set up an OAI interface, so that my content source can be indexed by BASE?

If you want to set up an OAI interface, look for the implementation guideline at the Open Archives Initiative's website. You can find more general information about OAI at OpenArchives.org and Wikipedia. With our OAI validator OVAL you can easily verify if your repository is compliant with the BASE requirements.

If your content source is an e-journal, it will be indexed by BASE automatically if an entry for your journal exists in the Directory of Open Access Journals (we index DOAJ's content regularly). You will find information about the procedure for getting a journal into DOAJ at the DOAJ-FAQ. You can also use the OJS software to provide your journal's content (in OJS an OAI interface is implemented). More information at the OJS website.

(5) How often do you update the content of indexed sources?

We are updating all indexed sources every weekend. In larger intervals all content is completely re-harvested and re-indexed.

(6) Why are some sources or some documents indexed incompletely?

If a data source is not indexed completely, this is generally related to trouble with the OAI interface of a data source. The web surface might be OK, but as we index OAI-metadata only, the web surface is not relevant for us. You can report errors via our contact form. If you are a manager of a repository, please check the compliancy of your repository using our OAI validator OVAL.

(7) Do you delete data sources from the index?

All data sources are checked regularly. If a data source is not working properly any more or doesn't offer any open access content, it is deleted from the index - temporarily or permanently.

4.3 Searching / Result List

(1) How do I search BASE?

See our search help.

(2) Do you offer a full text search in the indexed documents?

Due to time and performance constraints we are indexing only metadata (title, abstract...) of documents. Thus it's not possible to search the full text of the indexed documents.

(3) Can I narrow a search on open access content only?

After performing a search you can narrow your search on open access documents only. Click on "Access" in the "Refine Search Result" box. The result list will be narrowed on documents, which are clearly marked as open access documents by the data provider in their metadata. Keep in mind that only 30% of all indexed open access documents can be identified as open access because of lack of metadata information.

(4) Why can't I access the full text of a document?

About 60% of the indexed documents in BASE are open access, the rest are mere metadata entries without full text or can only be accessed, if you are authorized for accessing this particular data source. You can search the metadata of all indexed documents. The authorization is always done by the content provider. If you don't have access to a full text although your institution supposedly is authorized, please contact your IT department or the content provider.

(5) Why do I always end up with an error message when I try to access a document?

If you get an 404 error ("Page not found"), the web address (URL) of the document might have changed or the document was deleted since we indexed the repository recently. Though content from academic repositories should provide permanent addresses and changes or deletion of documents should be communicated via the OAI interface, in practice it's often not the case. Therefore it might happen that links to documents which appear on our result list do not work. Another reason for an error might be, that the server of the content provider is temporarily or permanently not available. If you encounter an error, please leave us a message. We will contact the content provider or remove the content source from our index, if it's a permanent problem.

(6) What are metadata?

Especially in an academic environment you will often come across documents containing metadata. These are descriptive elements assigned to a document in order to specify it both in technical respect and in terms of content. Metadata are for example author's names, publication dates, abstracts, language or - in case of a journal title - details regarding the title or the issue. If metadata are available, you may perform a targeted search for authors. In the result list you may refine the search result by categories.

4.4 BASE Website

(1) Why do I always end up on the German-language pages?

The BASE web pages are presented in the language, which is preselected in your browser settings. These settings can easily be changed (e.g. if you use the Mozilla "Firefox" browser, choose "Preferences" and then "Settings"). Switch to "English" as preferred language and the BASE pages will be presented in English immediately.

(2) Is there a print version of the BASE web pages available?

The BASE web pages are designed to automatically change

into a printer optimized version when the printing command is released.

(3) Is there an optimized version of the BASE web pages for mobile devices (smartphones etc.) available?

If you access BASE with a mobile device you will be automatically forwarded to the mobile version of BASE. You can access the mobile version directly at m.base-search.net.

(4) Do I have to enable Javascript, Java or something similar?

The BASE web pages are designed to show complete functionality without Javascript or Java.

(5) Are the pages "optimized" for specific browsers or browser versions?

There are no restrictions of any kind. The pages are properly designed according to web standards (XHTML, CSS) and comply with the WCAG regulations.

1 关于 BASE 搜索引擎

1.1 简介

BASE 是世界级海量内容的搜索引擎之一，专注于学术开放获取网络资源。比菲尔德大学图书馆负责 BASE 运营。

随着开放获取运动的发展壮大，越来越多的机构知识库服务器采取了“开放存储元数据收割协议”(OAI-PMH) 的方式提供内容。BASE 采集、标准化和索引化这些数据。BASE 提供超过来自 4000 个信息源（sources）的 8000 万份文献。

您能获取 60% 的经过索引后的文件全文。

本索引持续增强（continuously enhanced）更多 OAI 本地资源的整合。我们的博客（OAI-PMH Blog）交流有关 BASE 的收割和集成活动。

作为“欧洲科研的数字知识库基础设施愿景 (DRIVER) ”欧洲项目，BASE 是注册 OAI 服务提供者（OAI service provider）和贡献者。数据库管理者可以通过插件接口 (interface) 整合 BASE 的索引到您自己的本地基础设施（如元搜索引擎、图书馆目录等)。

1.2 特点

相较商业搜索引擎，BASE 具有如下特点。

①智能化选取资源。

②唯有符合学术质量和相关性等特殊要求的文件服务才被收录。

③一项数据资源列表（data resources inventory）提供了有关搜索方面的透明性。

④深入“底层网页”的网络资源，那些被商业搜索引擎所忽视或者被牺牲的资源。

⑤通过自动化的方法，进行元数据的修正、规范化和丰富化。

⑥搜索结果显示中，会包括之前的文献数据。

⑦显示某个文件的重用条件和获取。

⑧具有多个选项来排序搜索结果列表。

⑨具有“再定您的搜索结果（经过作者、主题、杜威十进分类法、出版年、出版类型、语言和文件类型）”的选项。

⑩能够以 DDC（杜威十进分类法）和文件类型进行浏览（Browsing）。

2 用户使用方式

2.1 浏览

0 Informatik, Informationswissenschaft,
1 Philosophie und Psychologie (561597)
2 Religion (184167)
3 Sozialwissenschaften (2767784)

不键入数据而发现文献。您能选择两种浏览方式，杜威十进分类法（DDC）和文献类型。

浏览 BASE（Start browsing BASE）。

2.2 同义词 / 翻译语

klimatologie
Exakte Suche
Zusätzliche Wortformen
Synonyme (Eurovoc The

与 Eurovoc thesaurus 进行多语言搜索：选择“多语言同

义词（Multilingual Synonyms）”，您能以同义词和翻译语进行搜索。在 Eurovoc 中有来自 21 国的超过 239 000 条术语。

与 Eurovoc thesaurus 进行搜索 （Search with Eurovoc）。

2.3 博客 / 推客

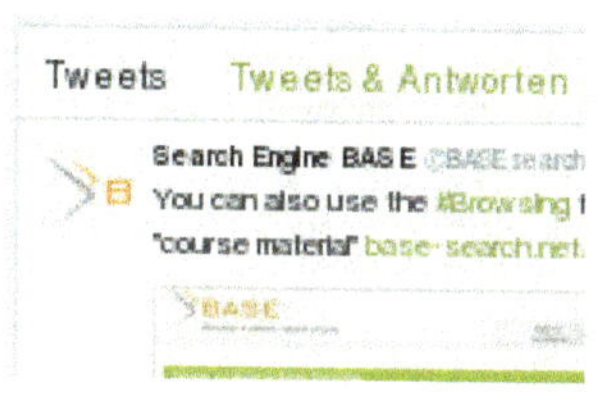

请加入我们的推客 @BASEsearch。如果您想推送 BASE 信息，您可使用 #basesearch，在我们的博客 Weblog 您能获得关于 BASE 的一般信息（仅限德语）。

2.4 移动通信设备的网页

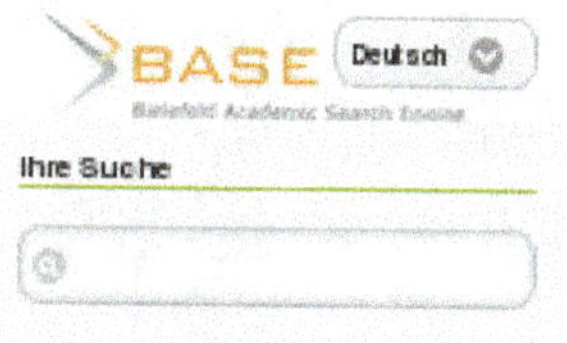

手机客户将被自动地指向我们的移动通信网址。BASE 支持所有现代化平台，如 Android、IOS、Windows 手机等。

访问移动通信网址（Access mobile website）。

2.5 搜索插件

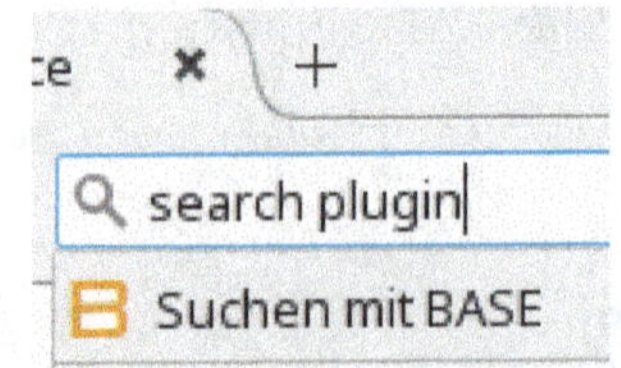

用 BASE 搜索插件会更快（提供 Firefox 2 和更高版本，以及 IE7 和更高版本）。您能在您的浏览器上通过搜索工具栏直接搜索 BASE 的学术网页。

安装 BASE 搜索插件（Install BASE search plugin）。

2.6 搜索框

如果您想在您的网页上提供 BASE 搜索的搜索栏位，简单地增加如下代码到您的主页即可：

<form action="http://www.base-search.net/Search/Results" method="get" accept-charset="UTF-8">

<input type="text" name="lookfor" style="width:200px;" maxlength="1024" />

<input type="submit" value="Search BASE" />

```
<input type="hidden" name="l" value="en" />
<input type="hidden" name="refid" value="dcexternen" />
</form>
```

利用 CSS 您能个性化设计搜索框，以便适用于您的网站。请小心不要改动代码，不然容易影响与 BASE 的互动功能。

2.7 Zotero 的界面

Zotero 是一项独立的开源软件的平台名称，该平台用作收集、管理和引用各种类型的线上和线下资源。它能够添加到火狐浏览器上。为实现可扩展性，它设定具有支持经典的参考文献管理系统的功能。在安装后，您可以转换 BASE 的搜索结果到 Zoetro 中应用。

下载 Zotero（Download Zotero）。

3 为数据库和知识库管理者服务

3.1 整合 BASE 到本地基础设施

```
<response>
 -<lst name="responseH
    <int name="status">
    <int name="QTime">
  -<lst name="params"
    -<str name="fl">
        dccollection,dccont
```

您能够整合 BASE 索引到您所拥有的本地基础设施上（如元搜索引擎、图书馆目录等）。为了能够实现，我们提供 HTTP 界面。您可下载操作手册：下载 BASE 界面手册（Download BASE Interface Guide）（手册 1.9 版，2016 年 6 月）。

您开始测试和使用界面之前，您的 IP 位置首先需要被注册。请发送给我们一段简短留言（message）。

3.2 BASE OAI 界面

```
<OAI-PMH xsi:schemaLoca
  <responseDate>2014-09-
  <request verb="ListRecor
- <ListRecords>
  - <record>
    - <header>
        <identifier>ftciteseer
```

您可以经由 OAI-PMH 接口，获取 BASE 索引：

BASE OAI 界面（BASE OAI interface）。

您开始测试和使用界面之前，您的 IP 位置首先需要被注册。请发送给我们一段简短留言（message）。

3.3 测试 OAI 界面

为知识库管理者的服务：OVAL 是 BASEOAI-PMH 测试器（BASE OAI-PMH Validity Checker），您能容易地测试是否符合 BASE 要求的 OAI 接口。

3.4 OAI-PMH 博客

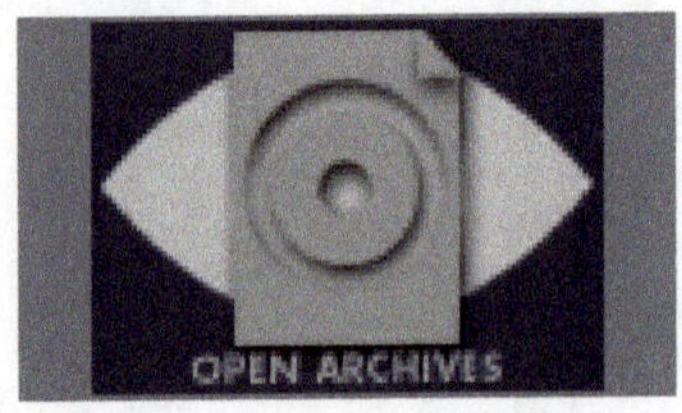

我们的 OAI-PMH 博客（OAI-PHM Blog）社群提供 BASE 收割和集成活动的信息。

4　常见问题

4.1　BASE 概述

（1）什么是 BASE？

BASE 是世界级海量内容的搜索引擎之一，专注于学术开放获取网络资源。比菲尔德大学图书馆负责 BASE 的运营。请尝试搜索 BASE 吧（searching with BASE）！

（2）什么是 BASE Lab（BASE 实验室）？

新的功能和工具将会在 BASE Lab 上首先公布。请点击我们的博客（Blog）或者推客（Twitter channel）更新。

（3）BASE 有什么不同？

BASE 能够高效率地、针对性地搜索与检索高质量学术信息。与谷歌或者必应等搜索引擎不同，BASE 具有这方面的深层网络搜索能力。在 BASE 中的信息源会被智能化挑选和评估，这就是为什么不会出现数据垃圾和邮件垃圾。

（4）BASE 背后的团队成员

BASE 由比菲尔德大学的 BASE（比菲尔德学术搜索引擎）小组所建立。

(5) BASE 的未来发展

战略项目 BASE 处于持续发展的状态。

(6) 请与我们联系！

我们高度重视您的评论和反馈。请给我们留言（message）、在博客上撰写评论（comment），或者在推客使用散类标签（#basesearch）。

4.2 索引 / 内容来源

(1) BASE 采用哪种索引软件？

自 2011 年 5 月起，我们使用 Solr/Lucene 的开源搜索技术。在 2011 年 5 月之前使用的是 Microsoft FAST（Fast Search And Transfer）的搜索引擎技术。

(2) 添加到 BASE 索引需要满足哪些要求？

我们索引所有类型的学术相关资源，以“开放存储元数据收割协议（OAI-PMH）”所提供的元数据（metadata）为基础。我们观察到一些知识库目录，如 OpenArchives、ROAR 和 OpenDOAR 等，以及知识库软件目录，如 DSpace 或 OJS 等，定期收割和索引这些信息源的内容。

(3) 我如何推荐一个新的内容信息源？

如果您是一位知识库管理者或者一份学术电子期刊的编辑，而您在我们的内容来源列表（list of content sources）中或者在索引中（search in our index）找不到您的内容来源信息，请通过“联系方式（contact form）”让我们知道：您的知识库名称、知识库主页的 URL 网址，以及 OAI 接口的基本 URL 信息。我们将立即确认数据，并且反馈您是否您的内容来源可被索引。

即使您不是知识库管理者，您也可以建议新的内容来源。该信息源必须包括学术文献及应该全文免费（开放获取）。请通过“联系方式（contact form）”发送它的名称和 URL 网址给我们，如果可能的话，包括 OAI 接口的基本 URL 信息。我们将确认内容来源是否符合我们的范围，并且反馈给您。

（4）我如何设定 OAI 接口，以便让我的内容来源能被 BASE 索引呢？

如果您想设定 OAI 接口，请见开放存储协议网站上的“安装指南（implementation guideline）”。您可以在 OpenArchives.org 和 Wikipedia 上发现更多有关 OAI 的一般信息。您可以容易地检查您的知识库是否符合 BASE 的要求（OVAL）。

如果您的内容来源是一份电子期刊，而且它在 DOAJ（Directory of Open Access Journals）上，则它将被 BASE 自动索引（我们定期索引 DOAJ 的内容）。您在 DOAJ-FAQ 上可发现注册到 DOAJ 上的程序。您也可以使用 OJS 软件来提供您的期刊内容（在 OJS 上实现 OAI 接口），这些信息可到 OJS website 上参考。

（5）你们多久更新索引来源后的内容？

我们每周更新所有索引来源。经过一段较大的时间间隔，所有内容都会完全重新收割和重新索引。

（6）为什么有些来源或者文献索引不完全？

如果数据源不被完全索引，通常与数据源的 OAI 接口出现故障问题有关。网页表面上看起来正常，但是我们只能索引 OAI 元数据（OAI-metadata）而不涉及资源的网页接口，因此出现不完全索引的情况时，希望您能通过“联系方式（contact form）”告知情况。如果您是知识库管理者，请用 OAI 检查器（OVAL）进行确认。

（7）你们会删除索引中的数据源吗？

所有数据来源都被定期检查。如果数据源工作不正常，或者不提供任何开放获取内容，它会被暂时或者永久删除。

4.3 搜索 / 命中列表

（1）搜索 / 命中列表

请见“BASE 使用说明（search help）”。

（2）我在已经索引的文献中可以搜索全文吗？

因为时效和功能等因素，我们只索引元数据（metadata），如文献的题名、摘要等，所以无法对文献进行全文搜索。

（3）我可以只搜索有开放获取内容的文献吗？

在执行搜索后，您可以缩小搜索范围只限开放获取内容。在“精炼搜索结果（Refine Search Result）”对话框中，点击“获取（Access）”。结果列表将被限定在那些数据提供者在元数据内注明为开放获取的文献。

（4）为什么我不能获取文献全文？

在 BASE 中经过索引的文献大约有 60% 可以开放获取，其他文献可能只有元数据，如果您有获取这些数据资源的授权则可以获取。您可以搜索所有经过索引的文献的元数据。授权许可取决于内容提供者。如果您的机构被授权而您不能获取，请您联系您的信息技术部门或者内容提供者。

（5）当我获取一份文献时，为什么最后经常显示“错误信息（Error Message）”呢？

如果您得到 404 error（“Page not found”）网页找不到，可能是文献的网页网址（URL）改变或者文献近期已被删除。经过学术知识库而来的内容，应该提供永久性网址，而且文献位置的改变或者删除应该会通过 OAI 接口传输，所以实际上这种情况不常发生。所以，一种可能是我们搜索结果列表中所显示的文献链接不可用，另一种可能是内容提供者的服务器当前或者长期失效。如果您遇到这个问题，请您给我们留言（leave us a message）。我们会与内容提供者取得联系，或者如果它长期有问题，我们就从索引中将其移除。

（6）什么是元数据？

特指在学术环境中，您经常与之沟通的文献的元数据。从技术层面和内容术语上，指对一份文献进行的一系列描述性指称。元数据，如作者姓名、出版日期、摘要、语言或者期刊名等，反映题名或者焦点议题的细节等。如果元数据可用，则您可以用作者等进行特定搜索；而在结果列表中，您可以利用分类目录来精炼搜索结果。

4.4 BASE 网站

（1）为什么我经常最后看到德文页面？

BASE 网页会根据您事先选定的浏览器设定来呈现。更改这些设定较容易[例如，如果您使用 Mozilla“火狐(Firefox)”的话，可以选择“性能（Preferences）”然后“设置（Settings）”等]。如果转换到“英文（English）”作为优先语言，则 BASE 网页就会立即呈现英文网页。

（2）BASE 的网站网页支持打印吗？

BASE 的网页设计是，当打印要求被传送时，会自动转换为打印版本。

（3）BASE 网站具有支持移动通信设备（如手机等）的优化网页吗？

如果您用移动通信设备，则 BASE 将自动为您切换到

BASE 移动通信版本。您也能够直接访问这个版本 m.base-search.net。

(4) 我需要安装 Javascript、Java 或者其他类似的软件吗?

BASE 网页设计为不需要用户安装 Javascript 或 Java 就能实现全部功能。

(5) BASE 对某些浏览器或者版本有网页"优化"版本吗?

BASE 不对任何类型浏览器或者版本进行限制。网页根据标准规范（XHTML、CSS）设计，并且符合 WCAGWCAG 规则。

5 中文版界面截图

5.1 搜索

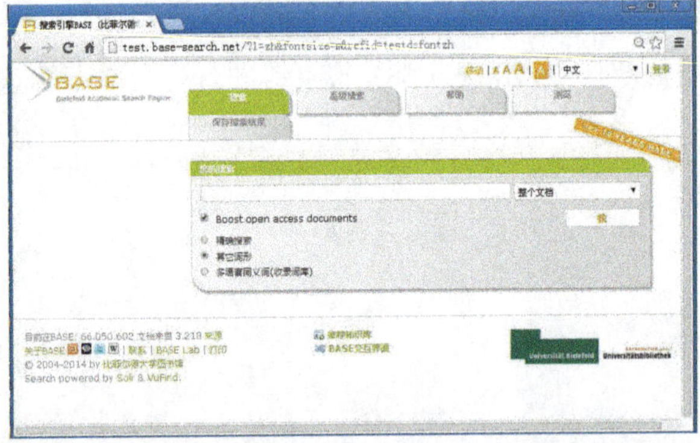

5.2 高级搜索

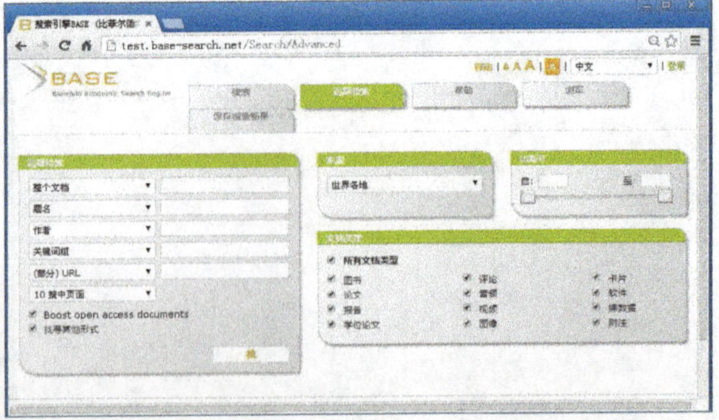

5.3 浏览

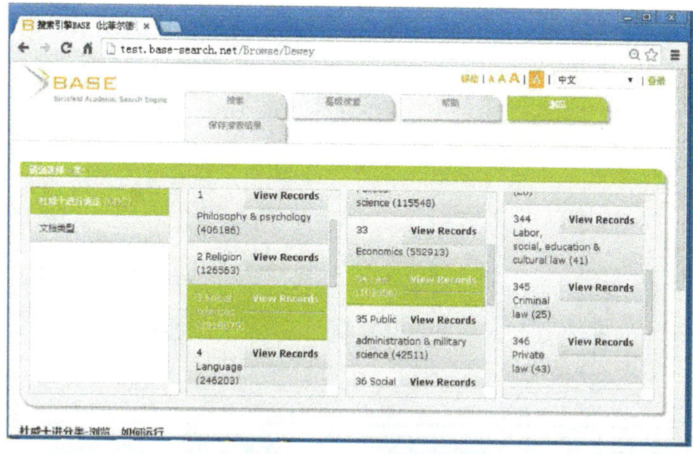

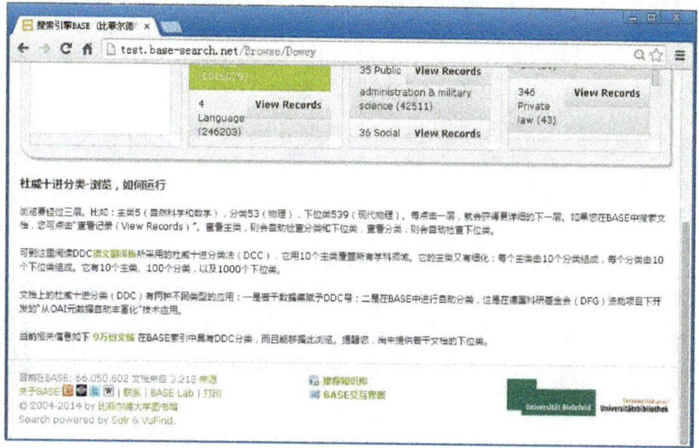

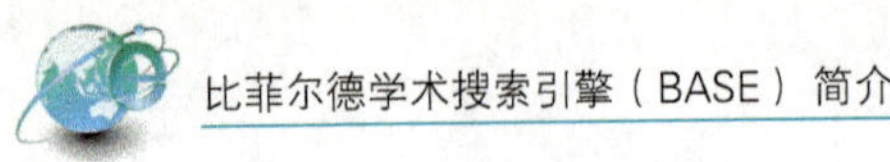

5.4 登录

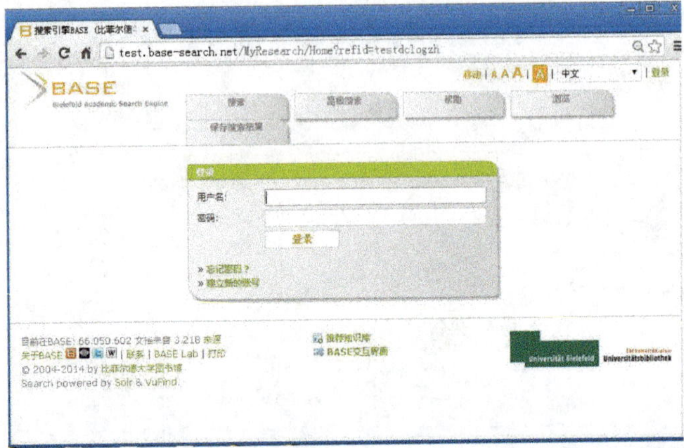

test.base-search.net/MyResearch/Home?refid=testdclogzh
中文
BASE
用户名:
密码:
登录
Search powered by Solr & VuFind.

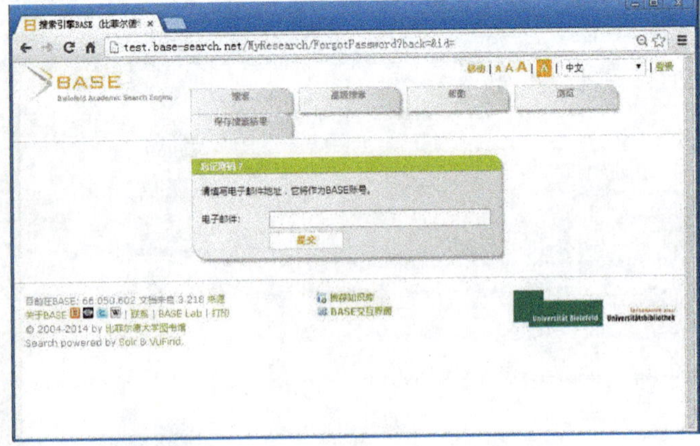

test.base-search.net/MyResearch/ForgotPassword?back=&id=
中文
BASE
电子邮件:
提交
Search powered by Solr & VuFind.

5.5 注册

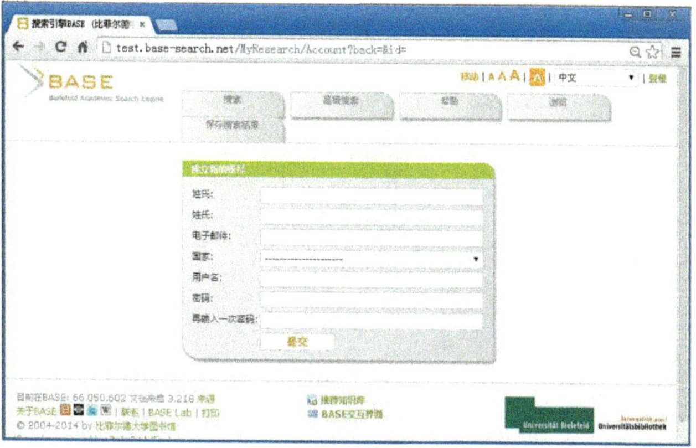
test.base-search.net/MyResearch/Account?back=&id=
BASE
中文
姓氏:
姓氏:
电子邮件:
国家:
用户名:
密码:
提交

5.6 收藏

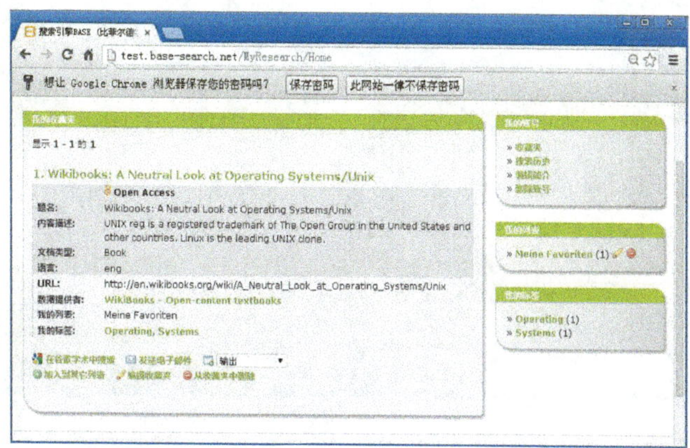
test.base-search.net/MyResearch/Home
想让 Google Chrome 浏览器保存您的密码吗?
保存密码
此网站一律不保存密码
显示 1 - 1 的 1
1. Wikibooks: A Neutral Look at Operating Systems/Unix
Open Access
题名:
Wikibooks: A Neutral Look at Operating Systems/Unix
内容描述:
UNIX reg is a registered trademark of The Open Group in the United States and other countries. Linux is the leading UNIX clone.
文档类型:
Book
语言:
eng
URL:
http://en.wikibooks.org/wiki/A_Neutral_Look_at_Operating_Systems/Unix
数据提供者:
WikiBooks - Open-content textbooks
我的列表:
Meine Favoriten
我的标签:
Operating, Systems
» Meine Favoriten (1)
» Operating (1)
» Systems (1)

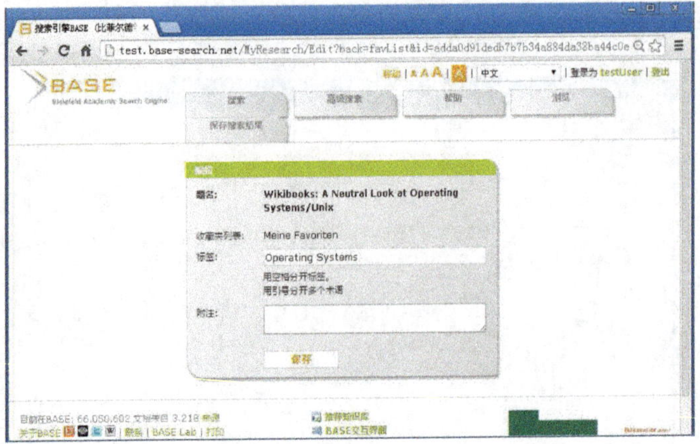
test.base-search.net/MyResearch/Edit?back=favList&id=adda0d91dedb7b7b34a884da32ba44c0e
BASE
题名:
Wikibooks: A Neutral Look at Operating Systems/Unix
Meine Favoriten
Operating Systems
保存

5.7 搜索结果与记录

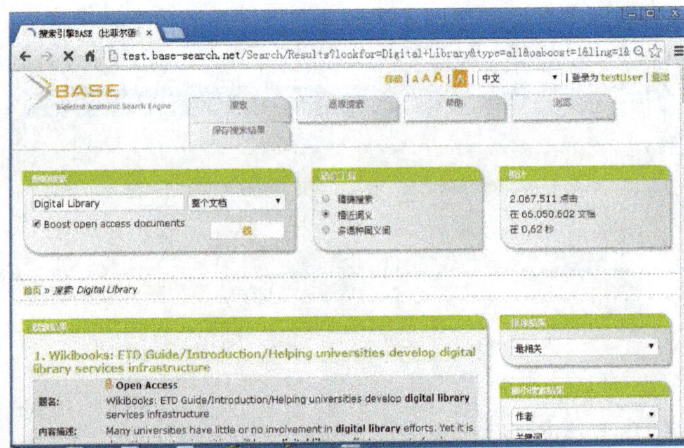
test.base-search.net/Search/Results?lookfor=Digital+Library&type=all&oaboost=1&ling=1&
BASE
Digital Library
整个文档
Boost open access documents
2.067.511 点击
在 66.050.602 文档
在 0,62 秒
Digital Library
1. Wikibooks: ETD Guide/Introduction/Helping universities develop digital library services infrastructure
Open Access
题名:
Wikibooks: ETD Guide/Introduction/Helping universities develop digital library services infrastructure
最相关
作者

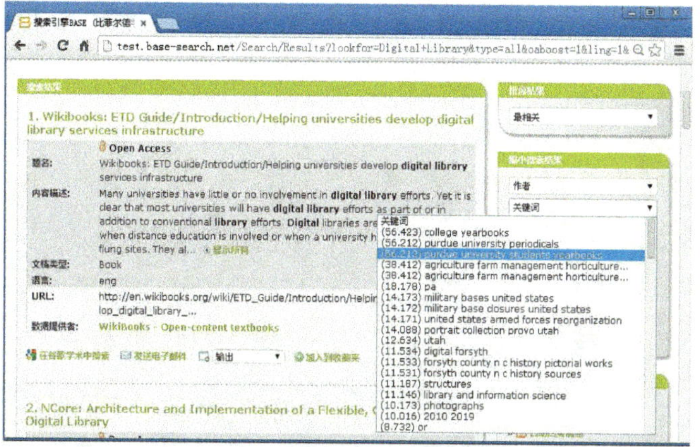
test.base-search.net/Search/Results?lookfor=Digital+Library&type=all&oaboost=1&ling=1&
1. Wikibooks: ETD Guide/Introduction/Helping universities develop digital library services infrastructure
Open Access
Wikibooks: ETD Guide/Introduction/Helping universities develop digital library services infrastructure
Many universities have little or no involvement in digital library efforts. Yet it is clear that most universities will have digital library efforts as part of or in addition to conventional library efforts. Digital libraries are
Book
eng
http://en.wikibooks.org/wiki/ETD_Guide/Introduction/Helping_universities_develop_digital_library_...
Wikibooks - Open-content textbooks
输出
最相关
作者
关键词
(56.423) college yearbooks
(56.212) purdue university periodicals
(38.412) agriculture farm management horticulture...
(38.412) agriculture farm management horticulture...
(18.178) pa
(14.173) military bases united states
(14.172) military base closures united states
(14.171) united states armed forces reorganization
(14.088) portrait collection provo utah
(12.634) utah
(11.534) digital forsyth
(11.533) forsyth county n c history pictorial works
(11.531) forsyth county n c history sources
(11.187) structures
(11.146) library and information science
(10.173) photographs
(10.016) 2010 2019
(8.732) or
2. NCore: Architecture and Implementation of a Flexible, Digital Library

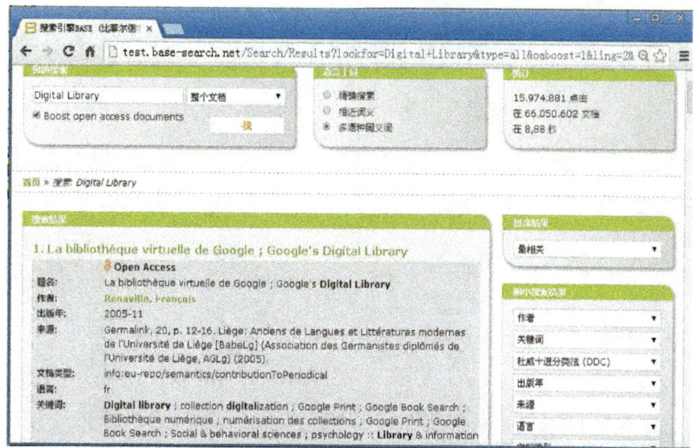
test.base-search.net/Search/Results?lookfor=Digital+Library&type=all&oaboost=1&ling=2&
Digital Library
整个文档
Boost open access documents
15.974.881 点击
在 66.050.602 文档
在 8,88 秒
首页 » 搜索: Digital Library
1. La bibliothèque virtuelle de Google ; Google's Digital Library
Open Access
La bibliothèque virtuelle de Google ; Google's Digital Library
2005-11
Germalink, 20, p. 12-16. Liège: Anciens de Langues et Littératures modernes de l'Université de Liège [BabeLg] (Association des Germanistes diplômés de l'Université de Liège, AGLg) (2005).
info:eu-repo/semantics/contributionToPeriodical
fr
Digital library ; collection digitalization ; Google Print ; Google Book Search ; Bibliothèque numérique ; numérisation des collections ; Google Print ; Google Book Search ; Social & behavioral sciences ; psychology :: Library & information
最相关
作者
关键词
杜威十进分类法 (DDC)
出版年
来源
语言

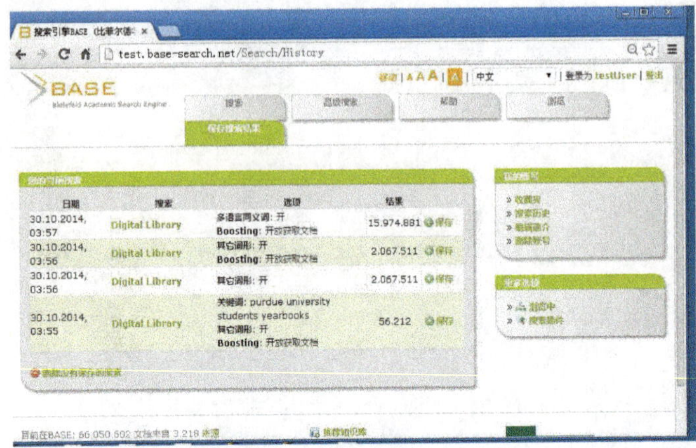
test. base-search. net/Search/History
BASE
中文
testUser
日期
搜索
选项
结果
30.10.2014, 03:57
Digital Library
多语言同义词：开
Boosting：开放获取文档
15.974.881
保存
30.10.2014, 03:56
Digital Library
其它词形：开
Boosting：开放获取文档
2.067.511
保存
30.10.2014, 03:56
Digital Library
其它词形：开
2.067.511
保存
30.10.2014, 03:55
Digital Library
关键词：purdue university students yearbooks
其它词形：开
Boosting：开放获取文档
56.212
保存

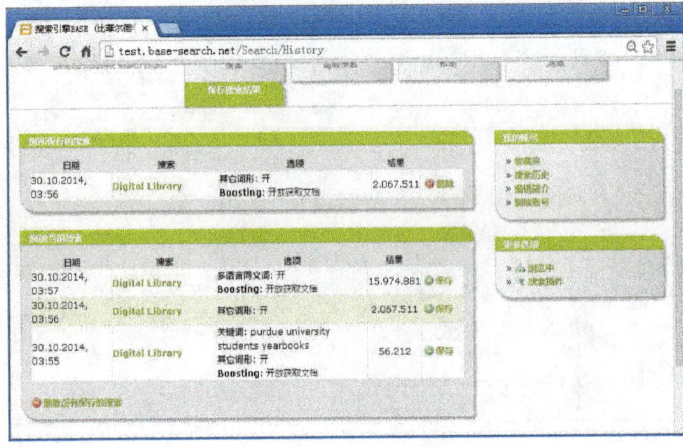
test. base-search. net/Search/History
日期
搜索
选项
结果
30.10.2014, 03:56
Digital Library
其它词形：开
Boosting：开放获取文档
2.067.511
删除
日期
搜索
选项
结果
30.10.2014, 03:57
Digital Library
多语言同义词：开
Boosting：开放获取文档
15.974.881
保存
30.10.2014, 03:56
Digital Library
其它词形：开
2.067.511
保存
30.10.2014, 03:55
Digital Library
关键词：purdue university students yearbooks
其它词形：开
Boosting：开放获取文档
56.212
保存

6 BASE HTTP 接口

BASE（比菲尔德学术搜索引擎，http://www.base-search.net/）标注网络资源及运用 DAI-PMH 收割科学知识库的元数据。它建立在开源搜索引擎软件 Lucene/SOLR 的基础上。近来 BASE 已经覆盖超过 2900 台文献服务器的百万文献量，而且整理为不同的典藏类型（请见内容来源列表 http://www.base-search.net/about/en/about_sources_date_dn.php?menu=2）。

BASE 的数据结构与索引结构相关，建立在 Dublin Core 及其扩展元数据的基础上。

BASE 提供 HTTP 应用程序界面。该界面受到 IP 控制，有兴趣的用户可以注册 http://www.base-search.net/about/en/contact.php。该界面的本地位置是：http://api.base-search.net/cgi-bin/BaseHttpSearchInterface.fcgi。

一旦注册（如一条 IP 地址或者已配置的范围），则能够轻易地在浏览器中编辑 URL 来测试（本地化在激活的 IP 范围内）并且寻求传递 XML 响应。

目前支持以下方法（Method）：

方法	描述
List Repositories	该方法列出所有可用的知识库或者知识库的存储数据集。该方法传递知识库的外部标识识别符等 XML 列表
List Profile	该方法列出包括 BASE 在内的知识库（由 BASE 识别符定义）的基本信息
Perform Search	这是界面的核心功能。它负责查询和传递正确结果。BASE 界面支持 SOLR 查询语法

6.1 ListRepositories

6.1.1 语法

<interface-url>?func=ListRepositories&coll=<collection_name>

参数	值	状态	描述
func	ListRepositories	mandatory	
coll	<collection_name>	optional	已存在的预先定义的集合：请见附录 1“涉及查询的集合”。必须要有存储数据集的名称，即便所有 BASE 的知识库都有列举

6.1.2 案例

（1）在欧洲的知识库

http://api.base-search.net/cgi-bin/BaseHttpSearchInterface.fcgi? func=ListRepositories&coll=ceu

响应：

```
<?xml version="1.0" encoding="utf-8"?>
<collection>
        <collection_name>ceu</collection_name>
        <list_repositories>
        <repository>
                <internal_name>ftabckrakow</internal_name>
        </repository>
        <repository>
                <internal_name>ftacademypublojs</internal_name>
        </repository>
        (...)
        </list_repositories>
</collection>
```

（2）在德国的知识库

http://api.base-search.net/cgi-bin/BaseHttpSearchInterface.fcgi? func=ListRepositories&coll=de

响应：

```
<?xml version="1.0" encoding="utf-8"?>
<collection>
```

<collection_name>de</collection_name>

<list_repositories>

<repository>

<internal_name>ftadwgoettingen</internal_name>

</repository>

<repository>

<internal_name>ftakai</internal_name>

</repository>

(...)

</list_repositories>

</collection>

（3）在德国的北莱茵西发利亚的知识库

http://api.base-search.net/cgi-bin/BaseHttpSearchInterface.fcgi? func=ListRepositories&coll=denw

响应：

<?xml version="1.0" encoding="utf-8"?>

<collection>

<collection_name>denw</collection_name>

<list_repositories>

<repository>

```
            <internal_name>ftbiecoll</internal_name>
        </repository>
        <repository>
            <internal_name>ftbietas</internal_name>
        </repository>
        (...)
        </list_repositories>
</collection>
```

6.2 ListProfile

6.2.1 语法

<interface-url>?func=ListProfile&target=<internal_name>

参数	值	状态	描述
func	ListProfile	mandatory	
target	<internal_name>	mandatory	由 ListRepositories 传递的个别知识库的对外名称

6.2.2 案例

知识库“ftbiecoll”的基本信息

http://api.base-search.net/cgi-bin/BaseHttpSearchInterface.fcgi? func=ListProfile&target=ftbiecoll

响应：

```
<?xml version="1.0"  encoding="utf-8"?>
<repository>
        <country>de</country>
        <name>Universität Bielefeld: BieColl - Bielefeld eCollections
</name>
</repository>
```

6.3 PerformSearch

PerformSearch 是搜索和检索 BASE 数据的本质方法。最新版本支持分页使用该新功能。

6.3.1 语法

```
<interface-url>?func=PerformSearch&coll=<collection>&query=<queryterm>&(...)
<interface-url>?func=PerformSearch&target=<internal_name>&query=<queryterm>&(...)
```

参数	值	状态	描述
func	PerformSearch	mandatory	
query	<queryterm>	mandatory	搜索术语：语法细节，请见附录 4“查询语法”
coll	<collection>	optional	为已经存在、预先定义的集合，请见附录 1“涉及查询的集合”

续表

参数	值	状态	描述
target	<internal_name>	optional	单一知识库的对外名称，以 ListRepositories 传递
hits	<number>	optional	每项响应的最大记录数据量（可以为零）。默认值为 10 笔
offset	<number>	optional	搜索结果的起始数量。默认值为 0 笔
sortby	<field+asc|desc>	optional	排序：排序规则必须包括一项单一栏目（请见附件 2 “栏目”，表格行列的 “排序” ），在空白键之后（如在 URL 的 + or %20）在排序目录之后 (asc or desc)。默认值为根据相关性排序
format	json	optional	设定响应形式为 JSON。默认值为 XML
fields	<field1,field2,...>	optional	该记录只包括列举在逗号分隔栏目列表中的栏位。已存在的预先定义的集合：请见附录 “涉及查询的集合”
facets	<field1,field2,...>	optional	该响应约束了从逗号分隔的分页列表中，抽取 “facet_counts/facet_fields” 的片段。该片段断开或者总结搜索结果。从用户角度，分页搜索打破搜索结果，而接触到多个分类结果，通常是逐一计数，而且允许用户 “钻取” 或进一步限制基于分页的搜索结果。利用分页并不影响搜索响应的结果。为已经存在、预先定义的分页

续表

参数	值	状态	描述
facet_ limit	<number>	optional	应当返回分页栏目的最大约束数量。默认值为 100 笔；最小 1 笔；最大 500 笔
facet_ sort	count | index	optional	分页栏目的排序方式包括：count – 数值排序（较高数值者排前）；index – 字母顺序排列。默认值为数值排列
f_<field> e.g. f_ dcsubject	<search_term>	optional	分页栏目的搜索术语。搜索结果可以被一些标准（分页）精炼

如果“target”或者“coll”有所缺失，而且“target”值不存在，则查询遍及全部 BASE 知识库。

6.3.2 案例

查询语法的细节，请见附录 4“查询语法”。

①文献来自“ftubbiepub”知识库，而且包括术语“lossau”和“summann”（在全部文献中搜索）：

http://api.base-search.net/cgi-bin/BaseHttpSearchInterface.fcgi? func=PerformSearch&target=ftubbiepub&query=lossau+summann

②文献来自意大利知识库，而且在 dccreator（作者）栏目包括术语“manghi”：

http://api.base-search.net/cgi-bin/BaseHttpSearchInterface.

fcgi? func=PerformSearch&coll=it&query=dccreator:manghi

③文献在 dccreator（作者）栏目包括术语“schmidt”及在 dctitle 栏目包括术语“biology”。该响应在 5 条记录之后，而且在 dctitle、dccreator 和 dcyear 栏目上命中数最多 5 条：

http://api.base-search.net/cgi-bin/BaseHttpSearchInterface.fcgi? func=PerformSearch&query=dccreator:schmidt+dctitle:biology&hits=5&offset=5&field s=dctitle,dccreator,dcyear

④文献包括术语“unix” 而且出版年份（dcyear）在 1983—2009 年的排序：

http://api.base-search.net/cgi-bin/BaseHttpSearchInterface.fcgi? func=PerformSearch&query=unix+dcyear:[1983+TO+2009]&sortby=dcyear+desc

⑤文献包括术语“unix”，其分页 dcsubject 和 dcyear 每个最大 10 条命中数（默认按照“Count”进行分页排序）：

http://api.base-search.net/cgi-bin/BaseHttpSearchInterface.fcgi? func=PerformSearch&query=unix&facets=dcsubject,dcyear&facet_limit=10

⑥文献包括术语“unix”及在 dcsubject 抽取术语“computer science”与在 dcyear 抽取“2008”，其分页 dcsubject 和 dcyear 每个最大 10 条命中数：

http://api.base-search.net/cgi-bin/BaseHttpSearchInterface.fcgi? func=PerformSearch&query=unix&facets=dcsubject, dcyear&f_

dcsubject=%22computer%20science%22&f_dcyear=2008&facet_limit=10

注意：搜索结果“query=unix+dcsubject:education”可以和分片页面搜索“query=unix&f_dcsubject=education”区别开来。在dcsubject栏目抽取术语“education”进行分页搜索，尽管纯粹的查询搜索会传递包括“education”在内的dcsubject栏目记录，栏位中的内容也会作为独立的关键词。例如“higher education”。

响应格式的案例：


```
<?xml version="1.0"  encoding="UTF-8"?>
<response>
<lst name="responseHeader">
        <int name="status">0</int>
        <int name="QTime">38</int>
        <lst name="params">
                <str name="facet">true</str>
                <str name="fl"> dccollection,dccontentty
pe,dccontinent,dccountry,dccreator,dcdate,dcdescription,dcd
ocid,dcdoi,dcformat,dcidentifier,dclang,dclanguage,dclink,dc
person,dcpublisher,dcrights, dcsource, dcsubject,dctitle,dcyear,d
ctype,dcclasscode,dctypenorm,dcdeweyfull,dcdeweyhuns,dcd
eweytens,dcdeweyones,dcautoclasscode,dcrelation,dccontribut
```

```
or, dccoverage,dchdate,dcoa</str>
                <str name="facet.mincount">1</str>
                <str name="facet.sort">count</str>
                <str name="q">creator:summann</str>
                <str name="facet.limit">10</str>
                <arr name="facet.field">
                    <str>f_dcsubject</str>
                    <str>f_dcyear</str>
                </arr>
                <str name="fq">collection:ftubbiepub</str>
        </lst>
  </lst>
  <result name="response"  numFound="23"  start="0">
        <doc>
                <arr name="dccontenttype"><str>application/
pdf</str></arr>
                <arr name="dclanguage"> <str>English</str>
</arr>
                <arr name="dclang"><str>eng</str></arr>
                <arr name="dcdoi">
                        <str>oai:pub.ub.uni-bielefeld.
```

de:1585315</str>

<str>urn:nbn:de:hbz: 361-11397</str>

</arr>

<arr name="dcclasscode"><str>020 </str>

</arr>

<arr name="dcdeweyhuns"><str>0</str>

</arr>

<arr name="dcdeweytens"><str>02 </str>

</arr>

<arr name="dcdeweyfull"><str>020 </str>

</arr>

<arr name="dcsubject">

<str>Digitalisierung</str>

<str>Altes Buch</str>

<str>Science General</str>

<str>ddc:020</str>

</arr>

<str name="dctitle">Digitisation of library collections in the Zips region (Slovakia)</str>

<arr name="dcformat"><str>application/pdf

</str></arr>

```
<str name="dccountry">de</str>
<str name="dccontinent">ceu</str>
<str name="dcsource"> Bibliometrics, 4 (3)
</str>
<date name="dchdate">2012-09-25T09:43:16Z
</date>
<str name="dcdate">2005</str>
<arr name="dccreator">
        <str>Summann, Friedrich</str>
        <str>Riedel, Susanne</str>
</arr>
<arr name="dcperson">
        <str>Summann, Friedrich</str>
        <str>Riedel, Susanne</str>
</arr>
<int name="dcyear">2005</int>
<int name="dcoa">1</int>
<arr name="dctype"><str>info:eu-repo/
semantics/article</str></arr>
<arr name="dcpublisher">
        <str>Bielefeld University Library
```

</str>

</arr>

<str name="dctypenorm">0001</str>

<arr name="dcidentifier">

<str>http://pub.uni-bielefeld.de/publication/1585315</str>

<str>http://pub.uni- bielefeld.de/download/1585315/2315313</str>

</arr>

<str name="dclink">http://pub.uni- bielefeld.de/publication/1585315</str>

<str name="dccollection"> ftubbiepub </str>

<str name="dcprovider">PUB - Publikationen an der Universität Bielefeld</str>

<str name="dcdocid">c6c24bdc6845a0f5e41647ece3b89d7e9d91270c0cd06a1492524ae83486ca88</str>

</doc>

(...)

</result>

<lst name="facet_counts">

```
    <lst name="facet_queries"/>
    <lst name="facet_fields">
        <lst name="f_dcsubject">
            <int name="science general">13</int>
            <int name="ddc 020">7</int>
            <int name="bielefeld academic search engine">6</int>
            <int name="ddc 004">6</int>
            <int name="communication"> 2</int>
            <int name="comunicazione"> 2</int>
            <int name="general works">2</int>
            <int name="informatica">2 </int>
            <int name="informatics">2 </int>
            <int name="informatik">2</int>
        </lst>
        <lst name="f_dcyear">
            <int name="2004">3</int>
            <int name="2005">3</int>
            <int name="2006">3</int>
            <int name="2009">3</int>
            <int name="1994">2</int>
            <int name="2012">2</int>
```

```
                    <int name="1976">1</int>
                    <int name="1988">1</int>
                    <int name="1998">1</int>
                    <int name="1999">1</int>
                </lst>
            </lst>
            <lst name="facet_dates"/>
            <lst name="facet_ranges"/>
    </lst>
    </response>
```

附 录

附录 1 涉及查询的集合

支持请求参数“coll”的值，以及“dccontinent”和“dccountry”的响应栏目。

代码	洲级区域
caf	非洲
cas	亚洲
cau	澳大利亚 / 大洋洲
ceu	欧洲
cna	北美洲
csa	南美洲
cww	网络服务器无关地理地域（国际组织）

国家地区（国家代码 ISO 3166）	
de	德国的知识库
nl	荷兰的知识库
uk	英国的知识库
etc.	……

德国国家区域情况	
debw	巴登 - 符腾堡州
deby	巴伐利亚州
debe	柏林
debb	勃兰登堡
dehb	不莱梅
dehh	汉堡
dehe	哈森
demv	梅克伦堡州 - 西波美拉尼亚
Deni	下萨克森州
Denw	北莱茵 - 威斯特法伦州
Derp	莱茵兰 - 普法尔茨州
Desl	萨尔
Desn	萨克森
Dest	萨克森 - 安哈尔特
Desh	石勒苏益格
Deth	图宾根

奥地利国家地区情况	
atb	Burgenland / 布尔根兰省
atk	Kärnten / 卡林希娅省
atnö	Niederösterreich / 下奥地利省
atoö	Oberösterreich / 上奥地利省
ats	Salzburg / 萨尔斯堡
atst	Steiermark/ 施蒂利亚省
att	Tirol / 蒂罗尔省
atv	Vorarlberg / 福拉尔贝格省
atw	Wien / 维也纳

瑞士国家地区情况	
chag	阿尔高
chai	阿尔卑斯山角内城
char	阿尔卑斯山角外城
chbe	伯恩
chbl	巴塞尔县
chbs	巴塞尔市
chfr	弗莱堡
chge	日内瓦
chgl	格拉鲁斯
chgr	格劳宾登

续表

瑞士国家地区情况	
chju	约拉
chlu	卢塞恩
chne	纳沙泰尔
chnw	瓦尔登
chow	奥布瓦尔登
chsg	圣加仑
chsh	沙夫豪森
chso	索洛图恩
chsz	施维茨
chtg	图高州
chti	提契诺州
chur	乌利
chvd	沃州
chvs	沃利斯
chzg	苏格
chzh	苏黎世

附录 2 栏目（用于搜索和响应）

作为请求参数的“查询”“栏目”“分页”“排序”等，以及作为内容的响应栏目。请注意打“×”的表示栏目有此参数。

外部栏目					
栏目	描述	状态	查询	分页	排序
dccollection	外部 BASE 知识库名称	single	×	×	
dchdate	更新 / 收割的数据	single	×		×

DC 元数据栏目（根据 Dublin Core 的定义）					
栏目	描述	状态	查询	分页	排序
dccontributor	贡献者	multi	×		
dccoverage	覆盖范围	single	×		
dccreator	作者	multi	×		×
dcdate	出版日期	single	×		
dcdescription	摘要	single	×		
dcformat	格式	multi	×		
dcidentifier	urls	multi	×		
dclanguage	语言	multi	×		
dcpublisher	出版者	multi	×		

续表

DC 元数据栏目（根据 Dublin Core 的定义）					
栏目	描述	状态	查询	分页	排序
dcrelation	关系	multi	×		
dcrights	权利	single	×		
dcsource	来源	single	×		
dcsubject	主题类别	multi	×	×	
dctitle	题名	single	×		×
dctype	出版和文献类型	multi	×		

Dublin Core 的扩展栏目					
栏位	描述	状态	查询	分页	排序
dcautoclasscode	杜威十进分类码（外部自动分类）	multi	×		
dcclasscode	得自文献元数据的 DDC 分类号	multi	×		
dccontenttype	内容类型	multi	×	×	
dccontinent	洲级区域（外部代码，请见附录 1“涉及查询的集合”）	single	×		
dccountry	国家代码 (ISO 3166)	single	×		
dcdeweyfull	DDC 分类号（原先自带 + 自动分类）	multi	×		

续表

Dublin Core 的扩展栏目					
栏位	描述	状态	查询	分页	排序
dcdeweyhuns	DDC 分类号（原先自带 + 自动分类）：百位数值	multi	×	×	
dcdeweytens	DDC 分类号（原先自带 + 自动分类）：十位数值	multi	×	×	
dcdeweyones	DDC 分类号（原先自带 + 自动分类）：个位数值	multi	×	×	
dcdocid	统一记录标识符（URI）	single	×		
dcdoi	外部 doi	multi	×		
dclang	规范化 DC 语言扩展元数据 (ISO 639-2/B: three-letter codes)	multi	×	×	
dclink	链接的首选 URL	single	×		
dcoa	开放获取文献 (0= 否，1= 是，2= 未知）	single	×		×
dcperson		multi	×	×	
dcprovider	内容提供者	single			

续表

Dublin Core 的扩展栏目					
栏位	描述	状态	查询	分页	排序
dctypenorm	得自 dctype（外部代码，请见附录 3“文献类型”）的出版物和文献类型的标准化格式	single	×	×	
dcyear	得自 dcdate 的年份标准化格式	single	×	×	×

附录 3　文献类型

在查询方面的代码，以及响应“dctypenorm”的栏目。

代码	描述
0000	文本
0001	期刊论文
0002	图书
0003	报告、白皮书、课堂材料
0004	论文
0005	评论
0101	音频
0102	视频
0103	图像

续表

代码	描述
0104	地图
0105	软件
0106	原始数据
0107	乐谱
9999	不知名材料

附录 4 查询语法

键入一个或者多个搜索栏目（用空白键分隔）将会减少反馈，因为会把所有键入的条目用于一份文献上（使用 AND 符号），所以越多选项合并到条目中，越会提升搜索效率。

您搜索…	举例	命中数
A and B	linear algebra	19 000
A and B as a phrase (directly adjoined)	"linear algebra"	6 000
A and/or B	linear OR algebra	575 000
A and B or A and C or A, B and C	algebra AND (linear OR numerical)	25 000
A and not B	algebra -linear	134 000
from A to B (only for numbers)	dcyear:[1983 TO 2009]	1 516 000

复数、词形变化和其他字形将被自动搜索。

符号*（星号）代表任意字符，而符号?（问号）代表一个字节。它们用来发现在不同语言上的单词所具有的不同拼写。如果您使用星号，系统将会停止对字形或者同义词的自动搜索。星号不能作为单词片语进行搜索。

例如：

搜索ho*e则回复记录有“home”“horse”“horticulture”等。

搜索ho？e则回复记录有“home”“hole”“hope”等。